donna hay

SIMPLE ESSENTIALS

chicken

thank you

Putting together a book is like doing one big jigsaw puzzle. When you begin there are ideas scattered here, concepts scattered there. Then it all starts to take shape and what once seemed impossible suddenly becomes reality. For helping to complete the final (beautiful!) picture I have so many people to thank: Vanessa Pitsikas, for being a designer wise, composed and talented beyond your years; recipe tester Jane Collings for dishes that elicit oohs and aahs every time; superlative copy editor Kirsty McKenzie for always asking the right questions; the amazing Con Poulos, talented Chris Court and all the other photographers whose images shine on every page; and, of course, to the *donna hay magazine* staff for being all-round superstars – your loyalty, creativity and professionalism help make donna hay a truly world-class brand. Many thanks must also be extended to Phil Barker and Peter Byrne at News Magazines; and to the team at HarperCollins. Thank you, thank you, thank you to friends old and new and my dear family. And to the men in my life: my extraordinary sons Angus and Tom who make my heart soar, and my partner Bill.

on the cover

front: crispy chicken salad, page 22
back: pan-fried chicken + bean salad with buttermilk dressing, page 72

Ecco

An imprint of HarperCollins*Publishers*

First American edition published 2008
First Australian edition published 2007
HarperCollins*Publishers*,
25 Ryde Road, Pymble, Sydney, NSW 2073, Australia
77-85 Fulham Palace Road, London W6 8JB, United Kingdom
2 Bloor Street East, 20th Floor, Toronto, Ontario M4W1A8, Canada
31 View Road, Glenfield, Auckland 10, New Zealand
10 East 53rd Street, New York, NY 10022, USA

Copyright © Donna Hay 2007. Design copyright © Donna Hay 2007
Photographs copyright © Con Poulos 2007 cover, pages 1, 4, 9, 10, 11, 12, 13, 14, 15, 16, 17, 19, 21, 23, 27, 30, 35, 37, 38, 39, 41, 42, 43, 45, 47, 49, 52, 53, 57, 61, 62, 63, 71, 73, 74, 75, 80, 85, 96, back cover; © Chris Court pages 7, 14, 15, 20, 24, 25, 29, 30, 31, 33, 51, 55, 56, 59, 61, 67, 69, 70, 81, 83, 87, David Matheson pages 42 (right), 49 (right), 77; Brett Stevens pages 65, 79 (right); Ben Dearnley page 67 (left); Lisa Cohen page 24 (right); Jonny Valiant page 79 (left)

Designer: Vanessa Pitsikas
Copy Editor: Kirsty McKenzie
Food Editors: Justine Poole, Steve Pearce, Jane Collings
Consulting Editor: Jana Frawley
Consulting Art Director: Sarah Kavanagh

Reproduction by Graphic Print Group, South Australia
Produced in Hong Kong by Phoenix Offset on 157gsm Chinese Matt Art. Printed in China.

HarperCollins books may be purchased for educational, business, or sales promotional use. For information in the USA, please write: Special Markets Department, HarperCollins Publishers Inc., 10 East 53rd Street, New York, NY 10022.

Library of Congress Cataloging-in-Publication Data has been applied for.

ISBN-13: 978-0-06-156901-2

First Ecco Edition 2008
08 09 10 11 /IMP 10 9 8 7 6 5 4 3 2 1

donna hay

SIMPLE ESSENTIALS

chicken

An Imprint of HarperCollinsPublishers

contents

introduction

It's far from accidental that chicken is one of the most popular meats on today's table. It's affordable, quick and easy to prepare and lends itself to a host of flavours and cooking techniques. Poaching, steaming, frying and roasting take you through the gamut of textures from comfort food tender to crisp and crunchy. Just about every cuisine has its chicken staple so we've taken a whizz around the world to come up with this selection from our favourite recipes. Variety, they say, is the spice of life, so join our cook's tour to see how easy it is to elevate an everyday food to the realm of the extraordinary.

Donna

basics

Perhaps the reason we all love chicken so much is not just
because of its versatility and ease of preparation but also
because you can make a meal from almost every part of
the bird. This is our definitive guide to the most popular
cuts in the Donna Hay kitchen along with basic recipes
for stocks, stuffings and cooking techniques which are
bound to become your most trusted stand-bys.

all about chicken

Whichever way you prepare it, chicken is a cut above other meats in terms of adaptability and speed of preparation. An everyday food in many cultures, it's little wonder that it was once treated as sacred.

breasts with part wing

Sometimes sold as supremes, this cut is absolutely failsafe for tenderness when briefly pan-fried to brown the skin side before finishing by roasting in the oven. Breasts with part wing are also great when you want to add flavours by inserting herbs, spices and other seasonings or stuffings between the skin and the flesh. They can also be completely cooked in a non-stick frying pan, provided you reduce the heat, cover the pan and cook slowly after the initial browning process.

drumsticks

A favourite with the young and young at heart, chicken drumsticks, or legs, can be fried, baked, casseroled or barbecued. They conveniently have a joint providing a natural grip for holding in one hand so they're also popular for picnics and parties where finger food is the order of the day. Drumstick meat is brown and tends to have a stronger flavour than the white meat cuts, so it's ideal for matching with robust seasonings such as chilli, honey and soy.

wings

Handy for use in soups and stocks, chicken wings can also be fried, baked, casseroled or barbecued. They say the meat that's closest to the bone is often the tastiest and certainly wings provide succulent morsels that readily take on marinating flavours and spices. You can also buy them as mini drumsticks with the tip removed and the meat pared back over the wing joint. The skin and fat content of wings mean they're not the first choice of slimmers.

maryland

Although the American state is known for its poultry production, it doesn't claim the dish or the cut as its own. In America, a maryland is fried chicken served with a cream sauce; in Australia, it describes a cut in which the thigh and leg are attached. Chicken marylands are conveniently serving-sized, and can be baked, fried or slow cooked in casseroles. Interestingly, the lunch menu on the *Titanic* featured chicken maryland.

skinless fillets

With skin removed and all fat trimmed, skinless fillets are a great option for people who are concerned about healthy cooking and fat counts. Fillets are cut from the breast or thigh and can be baked, steamed, casseroled or fried. They are the busy cook's greatest ally as they respond best to relatively short cooking times. Overcooked, they will be tough and shrivelled, so it's better to err on the side of less, rather than longer, cooking times.

whole chicken

Young chickens weighing somewhere between 1 and 1.5kg (2 to 3½ lbs) are tender and ideal for roasting whole or segmenting for pan or deep-frying. Older chickens of 1.5–2.5kg (3½–5½ lbs) often have more flavour but need gentler cooking by slow roasting or braising. Many people say that free-range chickens which are allowed to roam freely have better flavour than cage-reared birds. However, they are also more expensive.

all about chicken

butterflying

To reduce the time it takes to roast or grill (broil) a whole chicken, flatten it out. Take a sharp pair of kitchen scissors, cut along the backbone of the chicken, then press firmly on the breastbone to flatten it. This method, which is also called spatchcocking, allows you to flavour both the inside and outside of a bird with ease.

speedy solution

Another way to reduce cooking time is to butterfly whole chicken breasts. Take a sharp knife and carefully cut the breasts lengthwise but not all the way through. When folded out, the butterflied breasts will resemble a heart shape that's great for pan-frying, grilling (broiling) and barbecuing.

stuffing

Wash a 1.6–1.8kg (3½–4 lb) chicken (preferably fresh rather than frozen) and pat dry with absorbent paper. Spoon your choice of stuffing loosely into the cavity of the chicken. If the stuffing is packed too tightly, it won't heat all the way through. Using cotton string, tie the legs of the chicken together so that they are almost touching. This will help to keep the shape of the chicken while it is roasting, and will also prevent the stuffing from coming out of the cavity.

roasting times

Place the chicken on a rack in a roasting pan. Brush with oil and sprinkle with salt. Pour water or chicken stock into the base of the pan. Bake at 190°C (375°F) for 1 hour or until cooked (see chart below).

Roast in preheated 190°C (375°F) oven according to this size and time chart.

size	weight	time (min.)
14	1.4kg (3 lb)	50–55
16	1.6kg (3½ lb)	60
18	1.8kg (4 lb)	65–70

roasting tips

To test whether the chicken is cooked, skewer the flesh at the thickest point – under the leg, about 8cm (3 in) in, on the fleshy part of the thigh. The chicken is ready when the juices run clear, not pink. It's also important to check whether the stuffing is heated through properly. Push a metal skewer into the stuffing and hold there for 6 seconds; the part of the skewer in contact with the stuffing should become hot. Cook longer if it's only warm.

chicken essentials

chicken stock

Place 1.5kg (3¼ lb) chicken bones, 2 quartered onions,
2 quartered carrots, 2 chopped sticks celery, assorted herbs,
2 bay leaves, 10 peppercorns and 4 litres (128 fl oz) water in
a stockpot or large saucepan. Simmer for 3–4 hours, skimming
regularly. Strain and use, or refrigerate (for up to 3 days), or
freeze (for up to 3 months). Makes 2½–3 litres (80–96 fl oz).

steaming

This is a very healthy and gentle cooking technique which
is popular in Asian kitchens for preserving delicate flavours
and keeping chicken tender. Use a bamboo steamer lined
with baking paper, placed in a wok with a little water in the
base; or a two-tiered saucepan with a lid; or a colander over
a saucepan, with the lid covering the colander's contents.

poaching

The first rule of poaching is to keep it low and slow: turn down the heat and keep the liquid at a steady simmer. Poach a 150g (5 oz) chicken fillet for 8 minutes, then stand it in the poaching liquid for 15 minutes. Remove the chicken from the liquid and stand for 5 minutes before shredding or slicing. A larger 200g (7 oz) chicken fillet will need to stand longer.

pan-frying

Chicken breasts can be tricky to prepare; if you sear them over heat until they're cooked through, the outside can end up over-brown and tough. To cook breasts perfectly, brown them over high heat on both sides, then drop the temperature right down, put the lid on the pan and leave them to cook slowly.

chicken essentials

parmesan, pine nut + parsley stuffing

Combine 3 cups fresh breadcrumbs, ⅓ cup finely grated parmesan cheese, 3 tablespoons toasted pine nuts, ¼ cup chopped flat-leaf parsley and 20g (¾ oz) softened butter. Season with sea salt and cracked black pepper and mix until combined. You can vary the herbs, nuts and seasonings according to taste or the accompaniments for the chicken.

thyme butter

Combine 60g (2 oz) softened butter with 1 teaspoon chopped fresh thyme and sea salt and cracked black pepper. Carefully spoon the mixture in an even layer between the skin and the breast meat of a 1.6kg (3½ lb) chicken. Place on a greased rack and roast the chicken at 190°C (375°F) for 1 hour or until the juices run clear when tested with a skewer.

couscous stuffing

Combine 1 cup couscous with 1¼ cups (310ml/10 fl oz) boiling chicken or vegetable stock. Cover and stand until the stock is absorbed. Add ¼ cup chopped mixed fresh herbs (such as parsley, basil, chives, thyme or rosemary), 2 chopped cooked onions or leeks and cracked black pepper and sea salt and mix together well.

lemon and herb stuffing

Mix 3 cups fresh breadcrumbs with 2 teaspoons finely grated lemon rind, ¼ cup chopped mixed fresh herbs (such as parsley, basil, thyme, rosemary or chives), 60g (2 oz) soft butter, sea salt and cracked black pepper. Double the quantities for stuffing a large chicken or turkey.

17

starters, soups + salads

There are so many occasions when the mood, moment or appetite calls for a light, yet flavour-packed dish that will satisfy a craving or set the palate up for more substantial courses to follow. This selection of starters, soups and salads is as versatile as it is varied. With fresh flavour combinations and speedy preparation, the dilemma of what to serve for lunch, supper or first course has never been more easily resolved.

chicken and haloumi skewers

crispy chicken salad

Asian chicken noodle soup

chicken and haloumi skewers

48 oregano leaves

24 small bamboo skewers, soaked in water

250g (8 oz) haloumi cheese, drained and cut
    into 24 x 2cm (¾ in) cubes

2 x 200g (7oz) chicken breast fillets, cut into
    24 x 2cm (¾ in) cubes

1 tablespoon olive oil

1 tablespoon lemon juice

sea salt and cracked black pepper

lime or lemon wedges, to serve

Thread an oregano leaf onto a bamboo skewer, followed by a piece of haloumi, another oregano leaf and a piece of chicken. Repeat with the remaining skewers. Mix the oil, lemon juice, salt and pepper and brush over the skewers. Heat a non-stick frying pan over medium–high heat. Turn the skewers while cooking, for 2 minutes each side or until the chicken is cooked through. Serve with lime or lemon. Makes 24.

crispy chicken salad

¼ cup (60ml/2 fl oz) oyster sauce

1 tablespoon soy sauce

2 tablespoons plain (all-purpose) flour

cracked black pepper

4 x 140g (5 oz) chicken thigh fillets, thinly sliced

1 tablespoon olive oil

1 cucumber, thinly sliced

1 cup bean sprouts

1 cup coriander (cilantro) leaves

1 cup mint leaves

2 tablespoons lime juice

Preheat a medium non-stick frying pan over medium–high heat. Combine the oyster sauce, soy, flour and pepper. Add the chicken and toss to coat. Add the oil and chicken to the pan and cook for 2–3 minutes each side or until crispy and cooked through. To serve, toss the chicken with the cucumber, bean sprouts, coriander, mint and lime juice. Serves 4.

Asian chicken noodle soup

150g (5 oz) dried thin egg noodles

6 cups (1½ litres/48 fl oz) chicken stock

2 cups (500ml/16 fl oz) water

2 star anise (see glossary)

¼ cup (60ml/2 fl oz) soy sauce

1 cinnamon stick

3 slices ginger

2 x 200g (7 oz) chicken breast fillets

4 green onions (scallions), shredded

Place the noodles in boiling water and allow to stand for 5 minutes, then drain and set aside. Place the stock, water, star anise, soy, cinnamon and ginger into a saucepan over medium heat and cover. Simmer for 5 minutes. Add the chicken and cook for 5–7 minutes. Remove and shred the chicken. Return the chicken to the saucepan with the noodles and green onions. Cook for 3 minutes or until the noodles are heated. Serves 4.

cashew chicken salad with honey mustard dressing

1 cup raw cashew nuts

2 x 200g (7 oz) chicken breast fillets, sliced lengthways

sea salt and cracked black pepper

2 tablespoons olive oil

2 baby cos lettuce

honey mustard dressing

1 tablespoon Dijon mustard

2 tablespoons honey

1 tablespoon white vinegar

To make the honey mustard dressing, combine the mustard, honey and vinegar. Set aside.

Place the cashews in a food processor and process for 2–3 minutes. Coat the chicken with the cashews and salt and pepper. Heat a medium non-stick frying pan over medium–high heat. Add the oil to the pan and cook the chicken for 2–3 minutes each side or until cooked through. To serve, toss the chicken with the lettuce and spoon over the dressing. Serves 4.

cashew chicken salad with honey mustard dressing

chicken, leek and risoni soup

warm chicken and celeriac salad

chicken with spinach and white bean salad

chicken, leek and risoni soup

1 teaspoon oil
1 leek, sliced
1 x 200g (7 oz) chicken breast fillet, thinly sliced
4 cups (1 litre/32 fl oz) chicken stock
⅓ cup risoni or other small pasta
1 tablespoon flat-leaf parsley, chopped
sea salt and cracked black pepper
toasted Turkish bread, to serve

Heat the oil in a saucepan over medium heat. Add the leek and chicken. Cook for 2 minutes. Add the stock and pasta. Cook for 8 minutes or until the pasta is al dente. Stir through the parsley, salt and pepper. Serve with toasted Turkish bread, if desired. Serves 2.

warm chicken and celeriac salad

1 tablespoon olive oil
4 x 200g (7 oz) chicken breast fillets, trimmed
1 celeriac (650g/1 lb 7 oz), trimmed and peeled (see glossary)
125g (4 oz) baby spinach leaves
horseradish dressing
¼ cup (60ml/2 fl oz) olive oil
1 teaspoon fresh grated horseradish+
1 teaspoon caster (superfine) sugar
2 tablespoons lemon juice
sea salt and cracked black pepper

Preheat the oven to 200°C (400°F). Heat a non-stick frying pan over medium–high heat, add the oil and chicken and cook for 2 minutes each side or until browned. Place the chicken on a baking tray lined with non-stick baking paper, transfer to the oven and cook for 6–8 minutes or until cooked through. Allow to cool, then shred. Cut the celeriac into long, thin strips. Toss with the chicken.
   To make the horseradish dressing, place the oil, horseradish, sugar, lemon juice, salt and pepper in a bowl and whisk to combine. Pour the dressing over the celeriac and chicken and toss gently. To serve, divide the spinach between plates and top with the salad. Serves 4.
   + If fresh horseradish is unavailable, substitute 2 teaspoons of bottled grated horseradish or 2 teaspoons of horseradish cream.

chicken with spinach and white bean salad

4 chicken breast fillets, trimmed
olive oil, for brushing
sea salt and cracked black pepper
50g (1¾ oz) baby spinach, shredded
400g (14 oz) canned white (cannellini) beans, rinsed and drained
2 teaspoons white wine vinegar
1 tablespoon olive oil, extra
½ quantity aioli (recipe, page 88)

Heat a non-stick frying pan over medium-high heat. Brush the chicken with oil and sprinkle with salt and pepper. Cook the chicken for 5 minutes on each side or until golden and cooked through. While the chicken is cooking make the aioli. Toss the spinach with the white beans, vinegar, extra oil, salt and pepper. To serve, slice the chicken and serve with the spinach and white bean salad and aioli. Serves 4.

crispy chicken with pea salad

4 x 200g (7 oz) chicken breasts, skin on and trimmed
1 tablespoon olive oil
sea salt and cracked black pepper
⅓ cup (80ml/2½ fl oz) coconut milk
¼ cup chopped basil
1 garlic clove, crushed
200g (7 oz) sugar snap peas, trimmed and blanched
100g (3½ oz) baby spinach leaves

Preheat the oven to 200°C (400°F). Brush the chicken with the oil and sprinkle with the salt and pepper. Heat a medium non-stick frying pan over high heat. Cook the chicken, skin-side down for 3 minutes or until crispy, turn and cook for a further 3 minutes. Place the chicken on a baking tray lined with non-stick baking paper and cook in the oven for 5–6 minutes or until cooked through. Cut the chicken into pieces and set aside. Place the coconut milk, basil, garlic, salt and pepper in a bowl and mix well. Place the peas and spinach in a bowl, add the coconut mixture and toss to combine. Place the pea mixture on plates and top with the crispy chicken. Serves 4.

crispy chicken with pea salad

chicken coconut soup

1 cup (250ml/8 fl oz) chicken stock
2 x 400ml (14 fl oz) cans coconut milk
1 small piece ginger, sliced
1 stalk lemongrass, trimmed and halved
1 tablespoon store-bought red curry paste (see glossary)
4 x 200g (7 oz) chicken breast fillets, trimmed
250g (8 oz) vermicelli noodles
1 long red chilli, chopped
⅓ cup coriander (cilantro) leaves

Place the stock, coconut milk, ginger, lemongrass and curry paste in a saucepan over medium heat. Stir and bring to a simmer. Add the chicken and cook for 6–8 minutes or until the chicken is cooked through. Remove the chicken and shred. Set aside. Add the noodles to the soup and cook for 5 minutes. Place the noodles in bowls and spoon over the soup. Top with the shredded chicken, chilli and coriander. Serves 4.

chicken on lemongrass skewers

2 x 200g (7oz) chicken breast fillets, trimmed and chopped
1 tablespoon store-bought green curry paste (see glossary)
3 teaspoons fish sauce
2 teaspoons brown sugar
1 egg white
2 tablespoons finely chopped mint
8 lemongrass stalks, trimmed to 25cm (10 in) lengths+
2 teaspoons oil
sweet chilli sauce and lime wedges, to serve

Place the chicken, curry paste, fish sauce, sugar and egg white in a food processor and process until smooth. Stir through the mint. Refrigerate for 20 minutes. Line a baking tray with non-stick baking paper. Mould 2 tablespoons of the chicken mixture around 1 lemongrass stalk (use slightly wet hands for easier handling) and place on the baking tray. Repeat with the remaining mixture and lemongrass stalks. Refrigerate for 10 minutes or until needed. To cook, heat a large non-stick frying pan over medium–low heat. Add the oil and cook the skewers in batches, turning occasionally, until golden brown and cooked through. Serve hot or warm with chilli sauce and lime wedges. Serves 4.
+ Soak the lemongrass stalks in water for 20 minutes to prevent them from burning while cooking.

chicken coconut soup

chicken on lemongrass skewers

chicken and hoisin eggrolls   chicken noodle soup

chicken skewers with preserved lemon

chicken and hoisin eggrolls

4 eggs, lightly beaten
1 barbecue chicken, skin removed, meat shredded
1 cup mint leaves
1 cup coriander (cilantro) leaves
2 green onions (scallions), sliced
1 Lebanese cucumber, sliced
⅓ cup (80ml/2½ fl oz) hoisin sauce

Heat a small non-stick frying pan over high heat. Place ¼ cup (60ml/2 fl oz) of the beaten egg into the pan. Gently tip and swirl the pan so the egg covers the whole pan. Cook for 30 seconds or until golden. Set aside. Repeat 3 times with the remaining egg. Place the eggrolls on a board. Divide the chicken, mint, coriander, onion, cucumber and hoisin between each eggroll, placing it in the centre, and roll to enclose. Cut the rolls in half. Makes 8 pieces.

chicken noodle soup

1.6 kg (3¼ lb) chicken
11 cups (2¾ litres/88 fl oz) water
1 stick celery, finely chopped
1 carrot, finely chopped
1 onion, finely chopped
1½ cups macaroni or short soup noodles
2 tablespoons chopped flat-leaf parsley
toast, to serve

Preheat the oven to 200°C (400°F). Place the chicken on a greased rack in a baking dish, prick the skin all over and bake for 1 hour or until golden brown. Bring the water to the boil in a large saucepan over high heat with the lid on. Transfer the whole cooked chicken to the saucepan and add the celery, carrot and onion. Cover and cook for 15 minutes. Remove the chicken from the pan (reserving the cooking liquid) and allow to cool slightly. Remove and discard the skin, then remove the meat from the bones and chop. Skim any fat from the top of the stock, then strain the liquid and return to the pan. Place the chopped chicken and pasta in the pan and cook for 12 minutes or until the pasta is al dente. Stir through the parsley and serve with toast. Serves 4.

chicken skewers with preserved lemon

3 x 200g (7 oz) chicken breast fillets, trimmed and thinly sliced
2 tablespoons olive oil
½ cup preserved lemon rind, finely chopped (see glossary)
1 clove garlic, crushed
1 teaspoon dried chilli flakes
1½ tablespoons finely chopped thyme
1½ tablespoons finely chopped oregano
sea salt and cracked black pepper
25 bamboo skewers, soaked in water
whole-egg mayonnaise, to serve

Place the chicken, oil, lemon, garlic, chilli flakes, thyme, oregano, salt and pepper in a non-metallic bowl and mix well to combine. Thread the chicken onto the skewers. Cook on a preheated hot char-grill (broiler) for 1–2 minutes or until golden and cooked through. Serve with mayonnaise, if desired. Makes 25.

chicken salad with salsa verde dressing

4 bacon rashers, trimmed
4 x 200g (7 oz) chicken breasts
olive oil, for brushing
600g (1 lb 5 oz) baby/chat (new) potatoes, cooked and halved
1 bunch (100g/3½ oz) rocket (arugula)
salsa verde dressing
½ cup salsa verde (recipe, page 90)
1 tablespoon white wine vinegar
2 tablespoons olive oil

Heat a medium non-stick frying pan over high heat. Add the bacon and cook for 2–3 minutes or until browned and crispy. Set aside and keep warm. Brush the chicken with the oil and cook for 3–4 minutes each side or until cooked through. Slice the chicken and place in a bowl with the bacon and potatoes.

To make the salsa verde dressing, place the salsa verde in a bowl, add the vinegar and oil and whisk to combine. Pour the dressing over the chicken mixture and toss gently to combine. To serve, arrange on plates with the rocket. Serves 4.

chicken salad with salsa verde dressing

shredded chicken and mint noodle salad

200g (7 oz) bean thread or dried thin rice noodles+
3 x 200g (7 oz) cooked chicken breast fillets, shredded
1 cup shredded mint leaves
100g (3½ oz) beansprouts or snowpea (mange tout) sprouts
3 tablespoons sesame seeds
lime dressing
3 tablespoons fish sauce
2 tablespoons sugar
3 tablespoons lime juice
1 mild chilli, seeded and chopped

Place the bean thread noodles in a bowl and cover with boiling water. Allow to stand for 5 minutes, then drain. Toss the chicken with the noodles, mint, beansprouts and sesame seeds.

To make the lime dressing, combine the fish sauce, sugar, lime juice and chilli. Pour the dressing over the salad and chill until ready to serve. Serves 4.

+ If using rice noodles, cook in boiling water until al dente, drain.

Thai chicken san choy bau

1 tablespoon peanut oil
2 red chillies, chopped
500g (1 lb) chicken mince
2 tablespoons fish sauce
2 tablespoons lemon juice
1 tablespoon soy sauce
¼ cup chopped coriander (cilantro) leaves
¼ cup chopped mint leaves
baby cos lettuce leaves, to serve

Heat a medium non-stick frying pan over high heat. Add the oil, chillies and mince and cook for 5 minutes or until lightly browned. Add the fish sauce, lemon juice, soy and stir for 1 minute to combine. Remove the pan from the heat and stir through the coriander and mint. To serve, spoon the chicken mixture into baby cos lettuce leaves. Serves 4.

shredded chicken and mint noodle salad

Thai chicken san choy bau

pasta, noodles + rice

It's hard to imagine anything more deeply satisfying
than a bowl of pasta or noodles or the total comfort of a
creamy risotto. We've pared back the classics to make the
traditional favourites easier to prepare and taken a fresh
look at the produce department to help you create fresh
and flavourful dishes that are bound to have everyone
lining up for seconds. No one needs to know how fast
and simple they really are.

lemon chicken pasta

chicken, tomato and olive rigatoni   chilli cashew chicken noodles

lemon chicken pasta

400g (14 oz) spaghetti or linguine

3 tablespoons olive oil

3 tablespoons salted capers (see glossary), rinsed and drained

2 cloves garlic, sliced

2 small red chillies, seeded and chopped

3 x 200g (7 oz) cooked chicken breast fillets, shredded

1 tablespoon finely grated lemon rind

3 tablespoons lemon juice

1 cup chopped basil leaves

cracked black pepper

Cook the pasta in a saucepan of salted boiling water for 10–12 minutes or until al dente. Drain. While the pasta is cooking, heat a deep non-stick frying pan over high heat. Add the oil, capers, garlic and chillies and cook for 1 minute. Add the chicken and lemon rind and cook, stirring, for 4 minutes or until the chicken is heated through. Add the pasta to the pan with the lemon juice, basil and pepper and toss to combine. Place in serving bowls. Serves 4.

chicken, tomato and olive rigatoni

2 tablespoons olive oil

2 x 200g (7 oz) chicken breasts, thinly sliced

1 onion, finely chopped

2 cloves garlic, crushed

2 x 400g (14 oz) cans diced tomatoes

½ cup black olives

400g (14 oz) rigatoni, cooked and drained

sea salt and cracked black pepper

½ cup basil leaves

Heat 1 tablespoon of the oil in a non-stick frying pan over high heat. Cook the chicken for 2–3 minutes, or until cooked and golden. Remove from the pan and set aside. Heat the remaining tablespoon of oil in the pan on medium heat and cook the onion and garlic for 5 minutes until softened. Add the tomatoes and simmer, uncovered, for 10 minutes. Return the chicken to the pan with the olives and warm through. Toss the drained pasta with the sauce and season to taste. Top with basil to serve. Serves 4.

chilli cashew chicken noodles

2 tablespoons peanut oil

2 onions, sliced into wedges

4 large red chillies, seeded and chopped

¼ cup (55g/1⅞ oz) sugar

4 x 200g (7 oz) chicken breast fillets, sliced

1 red capsicum (bell pepper), sliced

¾ cup roasted unsalted cashews

2 tablespoons fish sauce

2 tablespoons soy sauce

2 tablespoons lemon juice

200g (7 oz) dried thick rice noodles, cooked and drained

¼ cup coriander (cilantro) leaves

Heat a wok or deep non-stick frying pan over high heat. Add the oil, onions, chillies and sugar and cook for 2 minutes. Remove from the pan and set aside. Add the chicken and cook, stirring, for 4 minutes or until the chicken is golden. Add the capsicum, cashews, fish sauce, soy, lemon juice, onion mixture and noodles. Cook, stirring, for 4 minutes or until heated through. Sprinkle with coriander. Serves 4.

chicken, chorizo and tomato paella

1 tablespoon olive oil

1 onion, finely chopped

2 cloves garlic, crushed

½ teaspoon paprika

2 x 100g (3½ oz) chorizo sausages (see glossary), sliced

2 x 200g (7 oz) chicken breasts, cut into large chunks

1½ cups medium-grain rice

400g (14 oz) can diced tomatoes

2 cups (500ml/8 fl oz) chicken stock

½ cup oregano leaves

2 cups baby spinach leaves

Heat the oil in a large frying pan over high heat. Add the onion, garlic, paprika, chorizo and chicken and cook for 5–10 minutes, until golden. Add the rice and tomatoes and stir to combine. Add the stock, reduce the heat to low, cover with a tight-fitting lid and cook for 15 minutes, or until rice is cooked. Stir through the oregano and spinach. Serves 4.

chicken, chorizo and tomato paella

pad thai

smoked chicken, lime and avocado pasta

Thai lemongrass rice salad

pad thai

300g (10½ oz) thick rice noodles, cooked and drained

2½ tablespoons peanut oil

2 eggs, lightly beaten

½ teaspoon shrimp paste (see glossary)

3 red chillies, chopped

3 x 200g (7 oz) chicken breasts, sliced

3 green onions (scallions), sliced

⅓ cup (80ml/2½ fl oz) fish sauce

⅓ cup (80ml/2½ fl oz) lime juice

1 tablespoon brown sugar

1½ cups beansprouts

¼ cup coriander (cilantro) leaves

¼ cup sliced garlic chives (see glossary)

¼ cup roasted unsalted peanuts, chopped

Combine noodles with 2 teaspoons of the oil and toss to coat. Heat 1 tablespoon of the oil in a wok or deep frying pan over high heat. Add the egg, swirl around and cook until just set. Remove and set aside. Add the remaining oil and the shrimp paste to the wok and cook for 1 minute or until fragrant. Add the chilli and chicken and cook for 3 minutes. Add the noodles, green onions, fish sauce, lime juice and sugar and cook for 3 minutes. Toss through the beansprouts, coriander, chives and cooked egg and sprinkle with the peanuts. Serves 4.

smoked chicken, lime and avocado pasta

¼ cup (60ml/2 fl oz) olive oil

1 tablespoon finely grated lime rind

2 tablespoons lime juice

sea salt and cracked black pepper

1 teaspoon caster (superfine) sugar

400g (14 oz) spaghetti, cooked and drained

200g (7 oz) smoked chicken, thinly sliced

2 cups baby rocket (arugula)

1 avocado, peeled and quartered

½ cup shaved parmesan cheese

Combine the oil, rind, juice, salt, pepper and sugar. Pour over the cooked pasta and toss to combine. Add the chicken and rocket and toss to combine. Serve with the avocado and parmesan. Serves 4.

Thai lemongrass rice salad

2 tablespoons peanut oil

2 stalks lemongrass, finely chopped

2 small red chillies, seeded and chopped

4 green onions (scallions), sliced

4 cups cooked long-grain rice

3 cups shredded cooked chicken

1 cup shredded mint

¾ cup coriander (cilantro) leaves

4 kaffir lime leaves (see glossary), shredded

3 tablespoons lime juice

1 tablespoon caster (superfine) sugar

2 tablespoons fish sauce

Heat a frying pan or wok over high heat. Add the oil, lemongrass, chilli and green onions and cook for 3 minutes. Place the rice, chicken, mint, coriander, lime leaves and lemongrass mixture into a bowl and toss to combine. Combine the lime juice, sugar and fish sauce and pour over the salad. Chill until ready to serve. Serves 4.

spaghetti with chicken and capers

200g (7 oz) spaghetti

2 x 200g (7 oz) chicken breasts, cooked and shredded

2 tablespoons lemon juice

2 tablespoons extra virgin olive oil

¼ cup chopped flat-leaf parsley

¼ cup chopped basil

1 tablespoon salted capers (see glossary), rinsed and drained

sea salt and cracked black pepper

grated parmesan cheese, to serve

Cook the pasta in a large saucepan of salted boiling water for 10–12 minutes or until al dente. Drain and return to the saucepan to keep warm. To serve, toss the chicken, lemon juice, oil, parsley, basil, capers, salt and pepper through the pasta. Serve with parmesan, if desired. Serves 2.

spaghetti with chicken and salsa verde

baked chicken and pumpkin risotto

2 cups arborio or carnaroli rice

5 cups (1¼ litres/40 fl oz) chicken stock

60g (2 oz) butter

700g (1½ lb) pumpkin, peeled and diced

1 tablespoon olive oil

3 x 200g (7 oz) chicken breast fillets

½ cup finely grated parmesan cheese

sea salt and cracked black pepper

2 tablespoons chopped flat-leaf parsley leaves

Preheat the oven to 190°C (375°F). Place the rice, stock, butter and pumpkin in an ovenproof dish and cover tightly with a lid or aluminium (aluminum) foil. Bake for 30 minutes or until the rice is soft. While the risotto is baking, add the oil to a non-stick frying pan over medium heat and cook the chicken for 4 minutes each side or until cooked through. Allow to cool slightly, then cut into chunks. Remove the risotto from the oven and stir in the chicken, parmesan, salt, pepper and parsley for 5 minutes, or until the risotto is creamy. Serve immediately. Serves 4.

stir-fried noodles with crispy chicken

200g (7 oz) dried Chinese wheat noodles

2 tablespoons peanut oil

2 large red chillies, seeded and chopped

2 tablespoons shredded ginger

600g (1¼ lb) gai larn (Chinese broccoli) (see glossary), sliced

3 tablespoons hoisin sauce

¼ cup (60ml/2 fl oz) soy sauce

1 tablespoon sugar

crispy chicken

4 x 200g (7 oz) chicken breast fillets, sliced

2 egg whites, lightly whisked

1 cup rice flour

2 teaspoons Chinese five-spice powder (see glossary)

1 teaspoon salt

peanut oil for shallow-frying

Cook the noodles in a saucepan of boiling water for 3 minutes or until soft. Drain and set aside. Heat the oil in a non-stick frying pan or wok over high heat. Add the chillies and ginger and cook for 2 minutes. Add the gai larn, hoisin sauce, soy and sugar and cook for 4 minutes or until the vegetables are tender. Toss through the noodles.

To make the crispy chicken, dip the chicken pieces into the egg white, then toss in the combined rice flour, five-spice powder and salt. Heat 1cm (½ in) oil in a medium non-stick frying pan over high heat and cook the chicken a few pieces at a time until golden. To serve, place the noodle and gai larn mixture on serving plates and top with the crispy chicken. Serves 4.

baked chicken and pumpkin risotto

stir-fried noodles with crispy chicken

baked chicken, lemon and pea risotto

2 tablespoons olive oil

3 x 200g (7 oz) chicken breast fillets, quartered

2 leeks, sliced

1 tablespoon lemon zest

2 cups arborio or carnaroli rice

5 cups (1¼ litres/40 fl oz) chicken stock

1½ cups fresh or frozen peas

2 tablespoons lemon juice

½ cup finely grated parmesan cheese

2 tablespoons chopped mint

sea salt and cracked black pepper

Preheat the oven to 200°C (400°F). Heat a non-stick frying pan over high heat. Add the oil and chicken and cook for 3 minutes on each side or until well browned. Set aside. Add the leeks and zest to the pan and cook for 5 minutes or until the leeks are softened. Place the leek mixture, rice and stock in a baking dish. Cover tightly with a lid or aluminium (aluminum) foil and bake for 20 minutes. Add the chicken and peas to the risotto, cover tightly and bake for a further 20 minutes. The risotto will still be quite liquid. Stir the lemon juice, parmesan, mint, salt and pepper through the risotto. Stir for 2 minutes to thicken the risotto and serve immediately. Serves 4.

chicken and mushroom macaroni

400g (14 oz) macaroni

1 tablespoon olive oil

1 brown onion, chopped

1 garlic clove, crushed

100g (3½ oz) swiss brown mushrooms, halved+

2 x 140g (5 oz) chicken thigh fillets, chopped

¾ cup (180ml/6 fl oz) (single or pouring) cream

½ cup (125ml/4 fl oz) chicken stock

sea salt and cracked black pepper

70g (2½ oz) baby rocket (arugula) leaves

¼ cup shaved parmesan cheese

Cook the pasta in a large saucepan of salted boiling water for 10–12 minutes or until al dente. Drain and keep warm. Heat a medium non-stick frying pan over high heat. Add the oil, onion and garlic and cook for 2–3 minutes or until the onion is softened. Stir in the mushrooms and chicken and cook for 3–4 minutes or until the chicken is golden. Add the cream, stock, salt and pepper and cook for 5 minutes or until slightly thickened. Add the chicken mixture to the pasta and toss to combine. To serve, stir the rocket into the pasta mixture and top with parmesan. Serves 4.

+ For a meatier taste, substitute large field mushrooms for the swiss brown mushrooms.

baked chicken, lemon and pea risotto   chicken and mushroom macaroni

roast + bake

The sheer genius of these dishes is that they require only brief preparation before leaving the oven to do the bulk of the work. That leaves you free to attend to the countless other tasks that await you when you get home from work and have a busy family life to contend with. To make life even easier, a number of these recipes can be served in the dish they're cooked in, for an added bonus of cutting down on the washing up.

glazed roasted spatchcocks

baked Italian chicken

chilli and lime quick flat-roasted chicken

glazed roasted spatchcocks

6 x 500g (1 lb) spatchcocks (see glossary), cleaned and dried
12 garlic cloves
12 rosemary sprigs
olive oil, for brushing
30g (1 oz) butter
redcurrant glaze
220g (7¾ oz) redcurrant jelly
1 tablespoon sherry vinegar

To make the redcurrant glaze, place the jelly and vinegar in a small saucepan over low heat and stir until the mixture is smooth. Set aside.

Preheat the oven to 200°C (400°F). Place 2 garlic cloves in each spatchcock cavity. Insert 2 sprigs of rosemary between the legs of each spatchcock and tie with kitchen string. Place the spatchcocks on a wire rack in a large baking tray, brush with the oil. Roast for 10 minutes or until just golden. Add the butter to the dish, brush the spatchcocks with the redcurrant glaze and roast for a further 20 minutes, brushing again with the glaze and melted butter after 10 minutes. Halve the spatchcocks and serve with pan juices. Serves 12.

baked Italian chicken

6 roma tomatoes, halved
3 teaspoons olive oil
sea salt and cracked black pepper
3 tablespoons store-bought pesto
4 x 200g (7 oz) chicken breast fillets
8 slices parmesan cheese
12 slices prosciutto (see glossary)
green salad, to serve

Preheat the oven to 200°C (400°F). Place the tomatoes, cut side up, in a baking dish lined with non-stick baking paper, drizzle with the oil and sprinkle with the salt and pepper. Bake for 20 minutes. Spread the pesto over the chicken breasts, top each with 2 slices of the parmesan and then wrap each in 3 slices of prosciutto. Place chicken in the baking dish with the tomatoes and bake for 10–15 minutes or until the chicken is cooked through. Serve with green salad. Serves 4.

chilli and lime quick flat-roasted chicken

1.8kg (4 lb) chicken
4 red chillies, seeded and chopped
2 tablespoons finely grated lime rind
2 tablespoons lime juice
1 tablespoon olive oil
sea salt
lime wedges, to serve

Preheat the oven to 200°C (400°F). Using kitchen scissors, cut along the backbone of the chicken, then press firmly on the breastbone to flatten it. Place the chicken in a baking dish lined with non-stick baking paper. Add the chillies, rind, juice, oil and salt and rub over both sides of the chicken. Bake for 35–45 minutes or until cooked through. Cut the chicken into segments and serve with lime wedges, if desired. Serves 4.

garlic pot-roasted chicken

1.6kg (3½ lb) chicken
1 lemon, peeled and thickly sliced
12 cloves garlic, unpeeled
8 sprigs thyme
12 baby/chat (new) potatoes
olive oil, for brushing
12 sage leaves
sea salt
1 cup (250ml/8 fl oz) chicken stock

Preheat the oven to 150°C (300°F). Wash and dry the chicken and place the lemon, garlic and thyme inside the cavity. Place in a large ovenproof pot with a lid. Place the potatoes around the chicken. Brush the chicken with oil and sprinkle with the sage and salt. Pour the stock into the bottom of the pot and cover with the lid. Bake for 1 hour. Remove the lid and bake for a further 30 minutes or until the chicken is golden and tender. To serve, slice the chicken, place on plates with the potatoes and spoon over the pot juices. Serves 4.

garlic pot-roasted chicken

ricotta and herb baked chicken

chicken breasts baked with lemon and fetta

harissa and yoghurt baked chicken

ricotta and herb baked chicken

¾ cup (190g/6¾ oz) ricotta
1 tablespoon finely grated lemon rind
1 tablespoon chopped basil leaves
1 tablespoon chopped oregano leaves
1 tablespoon chopped flat-leaf parsley leaves
sea salt and cracked black pepper
4 x 200g (7 oz) chicken breast fillets
400g (14 oz) can chopped tomatoes
2 cloves garlic, crushed
½ cup (125ml/4 fl oz) chicken stock
extra basil leaves, to serve

Preheat the oven to 180°C (355°F). Place the ricotta, rind, basil, oregano, parsley, salt and pepper in a bowl and mix well to combine. Use a sharp knife to cut a slit in the side of each chicken breast to create a pocket. Spoon the ricotta mixture into the pockets. Place the chicken in an ovenproof dish. Add the tomatoes, garlic and stock and bake for 25 minutes or until the chicken is cooked through. Sprinkle with basil to serve. Serves 4.

chicken breasts baked with lemon and fetta

2 tablespoons olive oil
1 tablespoon lemon juice
4 x 200g (7 oz) chicken breast fillets
⅓ cup basil leaves
2 tablespoons lemon zest
125g (4 oz) hard fetta cheese
cracked black pepper

Preheat the oven to 200°C (400°F). Place the oil and lemon juice in an ovenproof dish. Add the chicken and turn to coat in the marinade. Set aside for 5 minutes. Add the basil and zest then crumble over the fetta and sprinkle with pepper. Bake for 15 minutes or until cooked through. Serves 4.

harissa and yoghurt baked chicken

1.6 kg (3½ lb) chicken, quartered
1 tablespoon cornflour (cornstarch)
1 cup (250g/8 oz) thick plain yoghurt
1 tablespoon harissa or chilli paste
⅓ cup shredded mint
2 teaspoons ground cumin
green salad and lemon wedges, to serve

Preheat the oven to 200°C (400°F). Make deep slits all over the chicken pieces. Blend together the cornflour, yoghurt, harissa, mint and cumin. Spread the yoghurt mixture over both sides of the chicken. Place the chicken on a rack in a baking dish. Bake for 25–35 minutes or until the chicken is crisp and golden. Serve warm or cold with a green salad and a squeeze of lemon. Serves 4.

roast sweet potato and rosemary chicken

400g (14 oz) sweet potatoes (kumara), peeled and thinly sliced
¾ cup grated parmesan cheese
¼ cup (60ml/2 fl oz) olive oil
sea salt and cracked black pepper
1 tablespoon olive oil, extra
4 x 200g (7 oz) chicken breast fillets
½ cup (125ml/4 fl oz) chicken stock
1 teaspoon chopped rosemary
2 tablespoons wholegrain mustard
70g (2½ oz) baby spinach leaves

Preheat the oven to 180°C (350°F). Place the sweet potato, half the parmesan, the oil, salt and pepper in a bowl and toss until well combined. Layer the sweet potato on a baking tray lined with non-stick baking paper, sprinkle over the remaining parmesan and bake in the oven for 25 minutes or until golden. Heat a large non-stick frying pan over high heat. Add the extra oil and chicken and cook for 3 minutes each side. Place on a baking tray and cook in the oven for 10 minutes or until cooked through. Slice the chicken in half diagonally. Add the stock, rosemary and mustard to the frying pan and cook for 2 minutes. To serve, cut the sweet potato into squares, top with the spinach and chicken and spoon over the mustard mixture. Serves 4.

roast sweet potato and rosemary chicken

chicken pie

1 quantity shortcrust pastry (recipe, page 90)

375g (13 oz) store-bought puff pastry (see glossary)

1 egg, lightly beaten

filling

1 tablespoon oil

2 leeks, chopped

1kg (2¼ lb) chicken thigh fillets, cut into 2cm (¾ in) cubes

3 cups (750ml/24 fl oz) chicken stock

¾ cup (180ml/6 fl oz) dry white wine

250g (8 oz) small button mushrooms, halved

2 tablespoons chopped flat-leaf parsley

2 tablespoons cornflour (cornstarch)

¼ cup (60ml/2 fl oz) water

sea salt and cracked black pepper

To make the filling, cook the oil and leek in a saucepan over medium–high heat for 3 minutes or until soft. Add the chicken, stock and wine. Simmer, uncovered, for 45 minutes or until tender. Add the mushrooms and parsley to the pan and cook for 5 minutes. Blend the cornflour and water to a smooth paste, add to the pan and cook, stirring, for 5 minutes or until the mixture thickens and returns to a simmer. Add the salt and pepper. Set aside to cool.

Roll out the shortcrust pastry on a lightly floured surface until it is 3mm (⅛ in) thick and line the base of a deep 24cm (9½ in) pie tin. Spoon in the cooled filling. Roll out the puff pastry to 3mm (⅛ in) thick. Cut a slit in the middle of the pastry as an air hole. Place the pastry top onto the pie. Trim and press the edges together to seal and brush the top with a little egg. Bake at 180°C (350°F) for 40 minutes or until golden and crisp. Serves 6.

baked couscous with lemon and parsley chicken

olive oil, for frying

2 x 200g (7 oz) chicken breast fillets

2 cups couscous

2½ cups (675ml/20 fl oz) chicken stock

1 tablespoon olive oil, extra

sea salt and cracked black pepper

1 tablespoon finely grated lemon rind

¼ cup chopped flat-leaf parsley

2 tablespoons salted capers, rinsed, drained and chopped

½ cup black olives

Preheat the oven to 200°C (400°F). Heat a little oil in a non-stick frying pan and cook the chicken for 2 minutes on each side or until golden. Place the couscous in the base of a medium-sized baking dish. Pour over the combined stock, extra oil, salt and pepper. Place the chicken on top of the couscous. Combine the rind, parsley and capers and sprinkle over the chicken. Add the olives and cover the dish with a lid or aluminium (aluminum) foil. Bake for 20 minutes or until the chicken is cooked through. To serve, fluff the couscous with a fork, and spoon onto serving plates. Top with the chicken. Serves 2.

chicken pie

baked couscous with lemon and parsley chicken

quick flat-roasted chicken

classic fried chicken

green olive baked chicken

quick flat-roasted chicken

1.8kg (4 lb) chicken
1 lemon, sliced
8 sprigs thyme
6 cloves garlic, unpeeled
olive oil for brushing
sea salt and cracked black pepper

Preheat the oven to 200°C (400°F). Using kitchen scissors, cut along the backbone of the chicken, then press firmly on the breastbone to flatten it. Place the chicken in a baking dish lined with non-stick baking paper. Add the lemon, thyme and garlic. Brush with the oil, then sprinkle with salt and pepper. Bake for 35–45 minutes or until cooked through. Serves 4.

classic fried chicken

1.6 kg (3½ lb) whole chicken, cut into 8 pieces
2 cups (500ml/16 fl oz) buttermilk (see glossary)
peanut oil for deep-frying
flour coating
1¼ cups (190g/6¾ oz) plain (all-purpose) flour
1 teaspoon sea salt
½ teaspoon ground chilli
½ teaspoon cracked black pepper
1½ teaspoons Chinese five-spice powder (see glossary)

Place the chicken pieces in a bowl and pour over the buttermilk. Cover and refrigerate for 4 hours or overnight.

To make the flour coating, mix the flour, salt, chilli, pepper and Chinese five-spice in a bowl. Remove the chicken from the buttermilk and shake off any excess. Toss each chicken piece in the flour coating and set aside. Preheat the oven to 180°C (350°F). Heat the oil in a deep saucepan over medium–high heat. When hot, add the chicken pieces a few at a time and cook for 6–8 minutes or until a deep golden colour. As they are cooked, place the chicken pieces on a wire rack in a baking tray. When all the chicken is fried, place the tray in the oven and bake for 5–10 minutes to heat through. Serves 4.

green olive baked chicken

¾ cup pitted green olives, halved
1.6 kg (3½ lb) whole chicken
4 cloves garlic, peeled and halved
½ cup chopped flat-leaf parsley
2 tablespoons finely grated lemon rind
250g (8 oz) cherry tomatoes
2 tablespoons olive oil

Preheat the oven to 200°C (400°F). Soak the olives in cold water for 5 minutes to remove the excess salt. Drain. Divide the chicken into 8 pieces or ask your butcher to do so. Place the chicken in a baking dish, skin side up, and put a piece of garlic under each chicken portion. Combine the olives, parsley, rind, tomatoes and olive oil and spoon over the chicken. Bake for 45–55 minutes or until the chicken is golden and cooked through. To serve, place the chicken on plates and drizzle with the pan juices. Serves 4.

roast lemon and garlic chicken

2 garlic heads, halved
¼ cup (60ml/2 fl oz) olive oil
2 chicken breasts, trimmed
4 shallots, halved
4 quarters preserved lemon rind (see glossary), rinsed
2 tablespoons extra virgin olive oil
1 tablespoon white wine vinegar
200g (7 oz) green beans, trimmed and blanched

Preheat the oven to 180°C (350°F). Place the garlic in a baking dish with 1 tablespoon of the oil and roast for 5 minutes. Heat a medium non-stick frying pan over high heat. Add a tablespoon of the oil and the chicken and cook for 2 minutes each side or until browned. Add the chicken to the baking dish with the shallots and 2 preserved lemon pieces. Spoon over the remaining oil and roast for 8–10 minutes or until the shallots are tender and the chicken is cooked through. Finely chop the remaining preserved lemon, place in a bowl with the oil and vinegar and whisk to combine. Slice the chicken and arrange on plates with the roast garlic, shallots and beans. Spoon over the preserved lemon mixture to serve. Serves 4.

roast lemon and garlic chicken

crispy skin chicken with coriander salt and buttered carrots

4 x 350g (12¼ oz) chicken maryland pieces

1 tablespoon olive oil

1 tablespoon lemon juice

50g (1¾ oz) butter

1 cup frozen peas

1 bunch Dutch carrots, trimmed, peeled and blanched

coriander salt

1 tablespoon coriander (cilantro) seeds

2 teaspoons sea salt

To make the coriander salt, heat a small non-stick frying pan over high heat. Add the coriander seeds and cook for 1–2 minutes or until the seeds are light golden and fragrant. Place the seeds and the salt in the bowl of a small food processor and process until crushed. Set aside.

Score the skin of the chicken with a small, sharp knife and place in a non-metallic bowl. Add the oil and juice and marinate in the refrigerator for 30 minutes. Preheat the oven to 200°C (400°F). Heat a medium non-stick frying pan over high heat. Cook the chicken skin-side down for 3–4 minutes. Turn over and cook for a further 3–4 minutes or until golden. Place the chicken on a baking tray, sprinkle with coriander salt and cook in the oven for 15–20 minutes or until the chicken is cooked through. Add the butter, peas and carrots to the frying pan and cook for 3–4 minutes or until the peas are cooked. Spoon the vegetables onto plates and top with the crispy chicken. Serve with any remaining coriander salt. Serves 4.

lemon and honey roasted chicken

2 tablespoons lemon juice

¼ cup (60ml/2 fl oz) honey

2 tablespoons olive oil

sea salt and cracked black pepper

1 brown onion, cut into wedges

1.5kg (3 lb 5 oz) whole chicken, quartered

1 lemon, sliced

2 tablespoons rosemary leaves

Preheat the oven to 200°C (400°F). Place the lemon juice, honey, oil, salt and pepper in a small bowl and stir to combine. Place the onion, chicken, lemon and rosemary in a baking dish lined with non-stick baking paper. Brush the chicken with the honey mixture and roast for 45 minutes or until golden and cooked through. Serves 4.

crispy skin chicken with coriander salt and buttered carrots

lemon and honey roasted chicken

simmer, steam + stir-fry

When you need to whip up a quick supper after work
or a delicious dinner during a weekend on the run, the
techniques of the Asian kitchen are your greatest allies.
Not only are steamed and stirfried dishes speedy to
prepare, they also use minimal fat and provide maximum
preservation of flavour and nutrients. So you get to make
a stress-free meal that not only looks and tastes great
but is good for you as well.

chicken with cherry tomato and caper sauce

twice-cooked crispy chicken   gremolata seared chicken

chicken with cherry tomato and caper sauce

2 tablespoons olive oil

4 x 200g (7 oz) chicken breasts

2 cloves garlic, sliced

2 tablespoons salted capers (see glossary), rinsed and drained

250g cherry tomatoes, halved

sea salt and cracked black pepper

½ cup basil leaves

Heat 1 tablespoon of the oil in a large non-stick frying pan over medium heat. Add the chicken and cook for 4–5 minutes each side, or until cooked through. Remove the chicken from the pan and keep warm. Add the second tablespoon of oil to the pan over high heat and cook the garlic and capers for 1 minute, until capers start to pop. Add the tomatoes, salt and pepper and cook for 1–2 minutes, until tomatoes start to caramelise. Add the chicken back into the pan and toss to coat. To serve, sprinkle with basil leaves. Serves 4.

twice-cooked crispy chicken

¼ cup (60ml/2 fl oz) soy sauce

¼ cup (60ml/2 fl oz) Chinese rice wine (see glossary)

2 tablespoons brown sugar

1 cup (250ml/8 fl oz) chicken stock

2 star anise (see glossary)

1 cinnamon stick

4 x 200g (7 oz) chicken breast fillets, skin on

2 tablespoons peanut oil

steamed greens, to serve

Place the soy, wine, sugar, stock, star anise and cinnamon in a large non-stick frying pan over medium heat. Allow to simmer for 4 minutes. Add the chicken and cook for 3 minutes on each side. Drain the chicken on a wire rack and allow to dry. Heat a clean large non-stick frying pan over medium–high heat. Add the oil and the chicken, skin side down, and cook for 4 minutes or until the skin is very crisp. Turn and cook for 1 minute or until heated through. Slice and serve with steamed greens. For added flavour, pour some of the poaching liquid over the greens. Serves 4.

gremolata seared chicken

4 x 200g (7 oz) chicken breast fillets

2 tablespoons olive oil

roasted potatoes and steamed green beans, to serve

gremolata

½ cup finely chopped flat-leaf parsley

1 tablespoon salted capers (see glossary), rinsed and chopped

1 tablespoon finely grated lemon rind

To make the gremolata, combine the parsley, capers and lemon rind.

Sprinkle the chicken with the gremolata mixture. Heat the oil in a large non-stick frying pan over medium–low heat. Add the chicken and cook for 5 minutes on each side or until cooked through. Serve with roasted potatoes and steamed green beans, if desired. Serves 4.

pan-fried chicken and bean salad with buttermilk dressing

4 x 200g (7 oz) chicken breast fillets, trimmed

olive oil, for brushing

1kg (2¼ lb) baby/chat (new) potatoes, cooked and halved

300g (10½ oz) green beans, trimmed

300g (10½ oz) snow peas (mange tout), trimmed

1 fennel bulb, trimmed and thinly sliced

¼ cup mint leaves

½ cup (125ml/4 fl oz) buttermilk (see glossary)

2 tablespoons lemon juice

1 garlic clove, crushed

sea salt and cracked black pepper

Heat a medium non-stick frying pan over high heat. Brush the chicken with oil and cook for 3–4 minutes each side or until cooked through. Remove the chicken, set aside and keep warm. Add the potatoes to the frying pan and cook for 1 minute or until just golden. Cook the beans and snow peas in a saucepan of boiling salted water for 1–2 minutes or until just tender. Drain and refresh under cold water. Place in a bowl with the fennel, mint and potatoes and toss to combine. Whisk together the buttermilk, lemon juice, garlic, salt and pepper. Arrange the bean and potato mixture on plates, top with the chicken and spoon over the buttermilk mixture. Serves 4.

pan-fried chicken and bean salad with buttermilk dressing

poached chicken with coconut milk

lime and lemongrass chicken

crispy spiced Thai chicken

poached chicken with coconut milk

1¾ cups (14 fl oz) coconut milk
1¼ cups (10 fl oz) chicken stock
4 x 200g (7 oz) chicken breast fillets
2 sprigs coriander (cilantro)
1 stalk lemongrass, bruised
2 kaffir lime leaves (see glossary), crushed
2–3 tablespoons lime juice
1 tablespoon brown sugar
2 bunches (550g/1 lb 3 oz) gai larn (Chinese broccoli), blanched

Place the coconut milk and stock in a large, deep non-stick frying pan over medium–high heat and bring to the boil. Add the chicken, reduce heat and simmer for 15 minutes or until cooked through. Remove the chicken and set aside, keeping warm. Increase the heat to high, add the coriander, lemongrass and lime leaves and boil the coconut mixture for 10 minutes or until thickened. Stir through the lime juice and brown sugar. Remove the coriander, lemongrass and kaffir lime leaves and slice the chicken. Place the chicken on plates, spoon the coconut sauce on top and serve with the gai larn. Serves 4.

lime and lemongrass chicken

1 tablespoon olive oil
2 stalks lemongrass, shredded
4 x 200g (7 oz) cooked chicken breast fillets, thinly sliced
2 long red chillies, seeds removed and thinly sliced
¼ cup mint leaves
1 cos lettuce, leaves separated
¼ cup (60ml/2 fl oz) lime juice
2 teaspoons brown sugar
¼ cup (60ml/2 fl oz) fish sauce
2 limes, cut into wedges to serve

Heat a medium non-stick frying pan over high heat. Add the oil and lemongrass and cook for 2 minutes or until slightly softened. Combine the chicken, lemongrass, chillies and mint and spoon the mixture into the lettuce leaves. Place the lime juice, sugar and fish sauce in a bowl and whisk to combine. Spoon the lime mixture over the chicken mixture and serve with lime wedges, if desired. Serves 4.

crispy spiced Thai chicken

2 egg whites, lightly beaten
3 tablespoons rice flour (see glossary)
2 red chillies, seeded and finely chopped
3 tablespoons chopped coriander (cilantro) leaves
4 kaffir lime leaves (see glossary), shredded
3 tablespoons sesame seeds
3 x 200g (7 oz) chicken breast fillets, quartered
2–3 tablespoons peanut oil
watercress sprigs to serve
soy and lemon dipping sauce
3 tablespoons soy sauce
2 tablespoons lemon juice
1 tablespoon brown sugar

Place the egg whites, flour, chillies, coriander, lime leaves and sesame seeds in a bowl and stir until well combined. Add the chicken and toss to coat. Heat a non-stick frying pan over medium heat. Add the oil and cook the chicken for 3 minutes on each side or until golden and cooked through. Drain on absorbent paper.

To make the dipping sauce, place the soy, lemon juice and sugar in a bowl and mix to combine. Serve the chicken on some watercress with dipping sauce on the side. Serves 4.

chicken with preserved lemon mayonnaise

4 x 200g (7 oz) chicken breast fillets
olive oil, for brushing
sea salt and cracked black pepper
200g (7 oz) green beans, blanched
60g (2 oz) snow pea (mange tout) sprouts
1 quantity preserved lemon mayonnaise (recipe, page 90)

Brush the chicken with the oil and sprinkle with the salt and pepper. Heat a large non-stick frying pan over medium–high heat. Cook the chicken for 4–5 minutes each side or until cooked through. Toss together the beans and snow pea sprouts and serve with the chicken and preserved lemon mayonnaise. Serves 4.

chicken with preserved lemon mayonnaise

satay chicken

1 tablespoon oil
2 x 200g (7 oz) chicken breast fillets, sliced
1 long red chilli, thinly sliced
100g (3½ oz) snow peas (mange tout), trimmed
¼ cup (60ml/2 fl oz) coconut cream
1 tablespoon crunchy peanut butter
1 tablespoon soy sauce
¼ cup (60ml/2 fl oz) chicken stock
1 teaspoon fish sauce
2 tablespoons brown sugar
¾ cup coriander (cilantro) leaves
steamed rice, to serve

Heat a wok or large non-stick frying pan over high heat. Add the oil, chicken and chilli and cook for 2–3 minutes or until the chicken is golden. Add the snow peas and cook for 1 minute, then add the combined coconut cream, peanut butter, soy, stock, fish sauce and sugar and cook for a further minute or until slightly thickened. Stir through the coriander and serve with steamed rice. Serves 2.

chicken with green onion pesto

4 x 220g (7¾ oz) chicken breasts with part wing+, skin on
sea salt and cracked black pepper
1 tablespoon olive oil
200g (7 oz) green beans, blanched
2 cups frozen peas, blanched
1 cup chervil sprigs
green onion pesto
1 cup coriander (cilantro) leaves
4 green onions (scallions), chopped
1 clove garlic
3 teaspoons grated ginger
¼ cup (60ml/2 fl oz) olive oil
1 tablespoon soy sauce

To make the green onion pesto, place the coriander, green onions, garlic, ginger, oil and soy in a food processor and process for 1–2 minutes or until smooth. Set aside.

Place one tablespoon of the green onion pesto under the skin of each chicken breast and sprinkle with the salt and pepper. Heat a large non-stick frying pan over high heat. Add the oil and chicken and cook for 3–4 minutes each side or until cooked through. Combine the beans and peas in a large bowl. To serve, divide the bean salad between four plates and top with the chervil and chicken. Serve the remaining green onion pesto on the side. Serves 4.
+ Ask your butcher to trim and clean the chicken bone for you. This isn't essential to the recipe but it will look better on the plate.

satay chicken

chicken with green onion pesto

chicken and pumpkin stir-fry

soy-simmered chicken

lemon and garlic chicken parcels

chicken and pumpkin stir-fry

2 tablespoons peanut oil

2 onions, sliced

2 small red chillies, seeded and chopped

½ teaspoon cracked black pepper

4 x 200g (7 oz) chicken breast fillets, sliced

600g (1 lb 5 oz) pumpkin, peeled and thinly sliced

3 tablespoons fish sauce

¼ cup small basil leaves

Heat the oil in a preheated large non-stick frying pan or wok over medium–high heat. Add the onions, chillies and pepper and cook for 1 minute. Add the chicken and cook for 3 minutes or until browned. Add the pumpkin and fish sauce, cover and cook for 3–4 minutes, stirring occasionally, until the pumpkin is just soft. Stir through the basil. Serves 4.

soy-simmered chicken

2 teaspoons sesame oil

1 tablespoon shredded ginger

¼ cup (60ml/2 fl oz) soy sauce

1 tablespoon brown sugar

½ cup (125ml/4 fl oz) Chinese rice wine (see glossary)
    or dry sherry

2 star anise (see glossary)

1 cinnamon stick

4 x 200g (7 oz) chicken breast fillets

steamed greens and rice, to serve

Place the sesame oil, ginger, soy, sugar, wine, star anise and cinnamon in a frying pan over medium–low heat and bring to a simmer. Add the chicken and cook for 6–7 minutes each side or until cooked through. Place the chicken on plates and serve with the sauce from the pan, steamed greens and rice. Serves 4.

lemon and garlic chicken parcels

4 small potatoes, thinly sliced

4 sprigs rosemary

4 x 200g (7 oz) chicken breast fillets

3 tablespoons lemon zest

2 cloves garlic, crushed

1 tablespoon sea salt

1 tablespoon olive oil

Preheat the oven to 180°C (350°F). Cut out 4 pieces of non-stick baking paper each 30cm (12 in) square. Lay the potato slices down the centre of each of the paper pieces, leaving room at either end to fold. Place the rosemary on top of the potatoes and then top with the chicken. Combine the zest, garlic and salt in a small bowl and sprinkle over the top of the chicken. Drizzle with the olive oil. Fold the paper up to form sealed parcels around the chicken. Place the parcels on a baking tray and bake for 15 minutes or until cooked through. Serves 4.

cheese and olive crumbed chicken

3 cups fresh breadcrumbs

½ cup flat-leaf parsley leaves, chopped

1 cup grated cheddar cheese

¼ cup chopped black olives

½ teaspoon chilli flakes

4 x 200g (7 oz) chicken breast fillets, trimmed and sliced in half

plain (all-purpose) flour, for dusting

2 eggs, lightly beaten

2 tablespoons olive oil

2 vine-ripened tomatoes, sliced

150g (5¼ oz) green beans, blanched

1 tablespoon olive oil, extra

1 tablespoon lemon juice

Place the breadcrumbs, parsley, cheese, olives and chilli in a bowl and toss to combine. Dust the chicken with flour, dip in the egg and press into the breadcrumb mixture. Heat a non-stick frying pan over high heat. Add the oil and chicken and cook for 3–4 minutes each side or until cooked through and golden. Combine the tomatoes, beans, extra oil and juice in a bowl and serve with the chicken. Serves 4.

cheese and olive crumbed chicken

steamed ginger chicken

4 long slices ginger

4 x 200g (7 oz) chicken breast fillets

4 green onions (scallions)

1½ tablespoons soy sauce

1½ tablespoons fish sauce

steamed Asian greens, to serve

Place a slice of ginger on top of each chicken breast and tie with a green onion. Place the chicken on a plate with the ends of the green onion underneath. Combine soy and fish sauces, pour over the chicken and place the plate inside a large bamboo steamer over a large saucepan of boiling water. Cover and steam for 8 minutes or until cooked through. Serve with steamed Asian greens and drizzle with any juices. Serves 4.

Thai green chicken curry

2 teaspoons peanut oil

2–3 tablespoons store-bought green curry paste (see glossary)

500g (1 lb) chicken thigh fillets, quartered

1 cup (250ml/8 fl oz) coconut cream

¾ cup (180ml/6 fl oz) chicken stock

5 small slender eggplants (aubergines),
    cut into 2cm (¾ in) rounds

2 kaffir lime leaves (see glossary), shredded

1 long red chilli, seeded and finely sliced

1 bunch (250g/8 oz) snake beans, cut into 5cm (2 in) lengths

1 cup coriander (cilantro) leaves

steamed rice, to serve

Place a large saucepan over medium–high heat. Add the oil and curry paste and cook for 1 minute or until fragrant. Add the chicken and cook until browned. Add the coconut cream and stock and simmer, covered, over low heat for 20 minutes. Add the eggplants, lime leaves, chilli and beans and cook for 7–8 minutes or until the vegetables are tender. Stir through the coriander and serve with steamed rice, if desired. Serves 4.

steamed ginger chicken

Thai green chicken curry

glossary, index + conversions

aioli

1 egg
1 tablespoon lemon juice
3 cloves garlic, crushed
1 cup (250ml/8 fl oz) vegetable oil
sea salt

Process or blend the egg, juice and garlic in a food processor or blender until well combined. With the motor running, pour the oil in very slowly in a thin stream and process until the mixture is thick and creamy. Add salt. Makes 1¼ cups. For a quick cheat's version mix 1 cup of whole-egg mayonnaise with 2 cloves of crushed garlic.

arborio rice

Has a short, plump-looking grain with surface starch which creates a cream with the stock when cooked to al dente in risotto. Substitute with carnaroli rice.

Asian greens

These leafy green vegetables from the brassica family are now becoming widely available. We love their versatility and speed of preparation – they can be poached, braised, steamed or added to soups and stir-fries.

bok choy

A mild-flavoured green vegetable, also known as Chinese chard or Chinese white cabbage. Cook baby bok choy whole after washing it well. If using the larger type, separate the leaves and trim the white stalks. Limit the cooking time so that it stays green and slightly crisp.

choy sum

Also known as Chinese flowering cabbage, this Asian green has small yellow flowers.

The green leaves and slender stems are steamed or cooked in stir-fries.

gai larn

Also known as Chinese broccoli or Chinese kale, this leafy, dark green vegetable, with small white flowers and stout stems (the part of the plant that is most often eaten) can be steamed, blanched or stir-fried and served with soy sauce as a simple side dish.

garlic chives

Also known as Chinese chives, these have much flatter stems and a stronger flavour than Western chives. Trim the base end before use. Available from Asian grocers and some supermarkets.

balsamic vinegar

This Italian vinegar, although tart like other varieties, has a less astringent taste and more of a rich, red wine flavour. Like some wines, the older a balsamic vinegar is, the better it tastes.

blanching

A cooking method used to slightly soften the texture, heighten the colour and enhance the flavour of food such as vegetables. Plunge the ingredient briefly into boiling unsalted water, then remove and refresh under cold water. Drain well before using in salads or as a garnish.

broccolini

A cross between gai larn (Chinese broccoli) and broccoli, this green vegetable has long, thin stems and small florets. Available in bunches from supermarkets and greengrocers it can be substituted for broccoli.

buttermilk

Originally the name given to the slightly tangy liquid which was left over when cream was separated from milk, these days buttermilk is manufactured by adding cultures to low- or no-fat milk. Use in sauces, marinades, dressings and baking.

capers

Capers are the small, deep green flower buds of the caper bush. Available packed either in brine or salt. Use salt-packed capers when possible, as the texture is firmer and the flavour superior. Before use, rinse thoroughly, drain and pat dry.

celeriac

A root vegetable (also called celery root) with white flesh and a mild celery flavour. It is available in winter from supermarkets and greengrocers. Use in salads and soups or roast it with meats.

Chinese five-spice powder

This combination of cinnamon, Sichuan pepper, star anise, clove and fennel is excellent with poultry, meats and seafood. It is sold in Asian food stores and most supermarkets.

Chinese rice wine

Similar to dry sherry, Chinese cooking wine is a blend of glutinous rice, millet, a special yeast and the local spring waters of Shao Hsing, where it is made, in northern China. It is sold in Asian supermarkets, often labelled "shao hsing".

chorizo

Firm, spicy, coarse-textured Spanish pork sausage seasoned with pepper, paprika and chillies. Available from some butchers and most delicatessens.

fennel

With its mild aniseed flavour and crisp texture, fennel bulbs are ideal for salads or roasted with meats or fish. It's available from supermarkets and greengrocers.

fish sauce

An amber-coloured liquid drained from salted, fermented fish and used to add flavour to Thai and Vietnamese dishes. Available from supermarkets and Asian food stores, this pungent sauce is often labelled "nam pla".

green curry paste

Buy good-quality pastes in jars from Asian food stores or the supermarket. When trying a new brand, it is a good idea to add a little at a time to test the heat. Otherwise, make your own.

green curry paste recipe

½ teaspoon ground cumin
½ teaspoon ground coriander (cilantro)
¼ teaspoon ground turmeric
1 teaspoon shrimp paste
1 onion or 5 green onions (scallions), chopped
2 stalks lemongrass, white part only, sliced
4 kaffir lime leaves, shredded
2 teaspoons grated ginger
4 long green chillies (2 seeded), chopped
2 tablespoons chopped coriander (cilantro) root
¾ cup coriander (cilantro) leaves
2 teaspoons brown sugar
sea salt and cracked black pepper
2 tablespoons peanut oil

Place the cumin, ground coriander, turmeric and shrimp paste in a small non-stick frying pan over medium heat. Cook, stirring to break up the shrimp paste, for 2–3 minutes or until aromatic. Place the spice mixture in a food processor with the onion, lemongrass, kaffir lime leaves, ginger, chillies, coriander root and leaves, sugar, salt and pepper. Process until combined. With the motor running, gradually add the oil in a thin stream until the mixture is a smooth paste. Makes approximately 1 cup. Keeps in airtight container in refrigerator for two weeks.

haloumi

Firm white Middle Eastern cheese made from sheep's milk. It has a stringy texture and is usually sold in brine. Available from delicatessens and some supermarkets. Holds its shape during grilling and frying so is ideal for kebabs.

hoisin sauce

A thick, sweet Chinese sauce made from fermented soybeans, sugar, salt and red rice. Used as a dipping sauce or marinade and as the sauce with Peking duck. Available from Asian food stores and most supermarkets.

kaffir lime leaves

Fragrant leaves with a distinctive double leaf structure used crushed or shredded in Thai dishes. Available fresh or dried from Asian food stores and greengrocers.

lemongrass

A tall lemon-scented grass used in Asian cooking, particularly Thai dishes. Peel away the outer leaves and chop the tender root end finely, or add large pieces during

cooking and remove before serving. Available from Asian food stores, most supermarkets and greengrocers.

noodles

Like pasta, keep a supply of dried noodles in the pantry for last-minute meals. Fresh noodles will keep in the fridge for a week.

cellophane noodles

Also called mung bean vermicelli or glass noodles, these noodles are very thin and almost transparent. Soak them in boiling water and drain well to prepare them for soups and salads.

Chinese wheat noodles

Available dried and fresh in a variety of thicknesses from supermarkets and Asian food stores. Fresh wheat noodles need to be soaked in hot water before adding to stir-fries or cooked in boiling water. Dried noodles should be boiled before use.

fresh rice noodles

Available in a variety of thicknesses, including thin, thick and rolled, from the refrigerated section of Asian food stores and some supermarkets. Use noodles which are a few days old at the most, soak in hot water for 1 minute, then drain.

rice (stick) noodles

Fine, dry noodles that are common in Southeast Asian cooking. Depending on their thickness, rice noodles need only be boiled briefly, or soaked in hot water.

pancetta

A cured and rolled Italian-style meat that is like prosciutto but less salty and with a softer texture. It can be eaten uncooked.

pastry

Make your own or use one of the many store-bought varieties.

puff pastry

This pastry is time-consuming and quite difficult to make, so many cooks opt to use store-bought puff pastry. It can be bought in blocks from patisseries or bought in both block and sheet forms from the supermarket. You may need to layer several sheets together to achieve the desired thickness.

shortcrust pastry

A savoury or sweet pastry that is available ready-made in blocks and frozen sheets. Keep a supply for last-minute pies and desserts or make your own.

shortcrust pastry recipe

2 cups flour
145g (5 oz) butter
2–3 tablespoons iced water
Process the flour and butter in a food processor until the mixture resembles fine breadcrumbs. While the motor is running, add enough iced water to form a smooth dough. Knead very lightly then wrap the dough in plastic wrap and refrigerate for 30 minutes. When ready to use, roll out on lightly floured surface to 3mm (⅛ in) thick. This recipe makes 350g (12 oz), which will line up to a 25cm (10 in) pie dish or tart tin.

preserved lemon mayonnaise

½ cup (4 fl oz) mayonnaise
1 tablespoon lemon juice
1½ tablespoons salted capers,
    rinsed and drained
¼ cup chopped preserved lemon rind
⅓ cup chopped flat-leaf parsley
cracked black pepper
Place the mayonnaise, lemon juice, capers, preserved lemon, parsley and pepper in a bowl and stir to combine.

preserved lemon rind

Preserved lemons are rubbed with salt, packed in jars, covered with lemon juice and left for about 4 weeks. Remove the flesh and chop the rind for use in cooking. Available from delicatessens and specialty food stores.

prosciutto

Italian ham that has been salted and air-dried for up to 2 years. The paper-thin slices are eaten raw or used to flavour cooked dishes. Substitute with thinly sliced smoked bacon.

redcurrant jelly

This condiment has a slightly tart flavour. It is made from redcurrants, sugar and lemon juice. Available from specialty food stores and delicatessens, use it to flavour sauces for meat.

red curry paste

Buy good-quality pastes in jars from Asian food stores or the supermarket. When trying a new brand, it is a good idea to add a little at a time to test the heat as the chilli intensity can vary significantly. Otherwise, make your own.

red curry paste recipe

3 small red chillies
3 cloves garlic, peeled
1 stalk lemongrass, chopped
4 green onions (scallions), chopped
1 teaspoon shrimp paste
2 teaspoons brown sugar
3 kaffir lime leaves, sliced
1 teaspoon finely grated lemon rind
1 teaspoon grated ginger
½ teaspoon tamarind concentrate
2–3 tablespoons peanut oil
Place all the ingredients except the oil in the bowl of a small food processor or spice grinder. With the motor running, slowly add the oil and process until you have a smooth paste. Refrigerate in an airtight container for up to 2 weeks. Makes ½ cup.

rice flour

A fine flour made from ground white rice. Used as a thickening agent, in baking and to coat foods when cooking Asian dishes. Buy from supermarkets.

salsa verde

½ cup dill leaves
1 cup flat-leaf parsley leaves
½ cup mint leaves
2 tablespoons salted capers, rinsed
4 anchovy fillets, optional
1 garlic clove
cracked black pepper
2 tablespoons lemon juice
¼ cup (60ml/2 fl oz) olive oil
Place the dill, parsley, mint, capers, anchovies, garlic and pepper in the bowl of a small food processor and process in short bursts until roughly chopped. Add the juice and oil and process in short bursts until combined. Makes ½ cup.

shrimp paste

Also called blachan, this strong-smelling paste is made from salted and fermented dried shrimps pounded with salt. Used in Southeast Asian dishes. Keep sealed in the fridge and fry before using. Available from Asian food stores.

spatchcock

Originally a cooking term describing the process of butterflying, or splitting poultry along the backbone and flattening for grilling or roasting. The term has evolved to describe a very small chicken, which is frequently prepared in this manner. Weighing around 500g (1 lb), these small birds are sometimes called by their French name, poussin.

star anise

Small, brown seed-cluster that is shaped like a star. It has a strong aniseed flavour that can be used whole or ground in sweet and savoury dishes. Available from supermarkets and specialty food stores.

sweet potato

Long, tuberous root available in white and red or orange fleshed varieties. The red sweet potato, also known as kumara, is sweeter and moister. Both varieties can be roasted, boiled and mashed. Although different from the yam, they can be cooked in the same way.

white beans

These small, kidney-shaped beans are also often called cannellini beans. Available from delicatessens and supermarkets either canned or in dried form. Dried beans need to be soaked overnight before cooking.

conversion chart

1 teaspoon = 5ml
1 Australian tablespoon = 20ml (4 teaspoons)
1 UK tablespoon = 15ml (3 teaspoons/½ fl oz)
1 cup = 250ml (8 fl oz)

liquid conversions

metric	imperial	cups
30ml	1 fl oz	⅛ cup
60ml	2 fl oz	¼ cup
80ml	2½ fl oz	⅓ cup
125ml	4 fl oz	½ cup
185ml	6 fl oz	¾ cup
250ml	8 fl oz	1 cup
375ml	12 fl oz	1½ cups
500ml	16 fl oz	2 cups
600ml	20 fl oz	2½ cups
750ml	24 fl oz	3 cups
1 litre	32 fl oz	4 cups

cup measures

1 cup sugar, brown	175g	6 oz
1 cup caster (superfine) sugar	220g	7¾ oz
1 cup plain (all-purpose) flour	150g	5¼ oz
1 cup rice flour	100g	3½ oz
1 cup rice, cooked	165g	5¾ oz
1 cup arborio rice, uncooked	220g	7¾ oz
1 cup couscous, uncooked	180g	6¼ oz
1 cup basil leaves	45g	1⅔ oz
1 cup coriander (cilantro) leaves	40g	1½ oz
1 cup mint leaves	35g	1¼ oz
1 cup flat-leaf parsley leaves	40g	1½ oz
1 cup cashews, whole	150g	5¼ oz
1 cup cooked chicken, shredded	150g	5¼ oz
1 cup olives	175g	6 oz
1 cup parmesan cheese, finely grated	100g	3½ oz
1 cup green peas, frozen	170g	5¾ oz

If you love the great recipes in this book,
you'll love *donna hay magazine*

donna hay magazine features fresh, modern recipes
and styling ideas for every day and special occasions

special made simple

donna hay
magazine

At the age of eight, Donna Hay put on an apron and never looked back. She completed formal training in home economics at technical college then moved to the world of magazine test kitchens and publishing where she established her trademark style of simple, smart and seasonal recipes all beautifully put together and photographed. It is food for every cook, every food lover, every day and every occasion. And, it is the style that turned her into an international food publishing phenomenon as a bestselling author, publisher of *donna hay magazine*, newspaper columnist, and creator of a homewares and food range.

books by Donna Hay: *off the shelf, modern classics book 1, modern classics book 2, the instant cook,* and *instant entertaining,* plus more.